Our Country's Holidays

Fourth of July

by Sheri Dean

Reading consultant: Susan Nations, M.Ed.,
author/literacy coach/
consultant in literacy development

Please visit our web site at: www.earlyliteracy.cc
For a free color catalog describing Weekly Reader® Early Learning Library's list
of high-quality books, call 1-877-445-5824 (USA) or 1-800-387-3178 (Canada).
Weekly Reader® Early Learning Library's fax: (414) 336-0164.

Library of Congress Cataloging-in-Publication Data available upon request from publisher.
Fax (414) 336-0157 for the attention of the Publishing Records Department.

ISBN 0-8368-6505-7 (lib. bdg.)
ISBN 0-8368-6512-X (softcover)

This edition first published in 2006 by
Weekly Reader® Early Learning Library
A Member of the WRC Media Family of Companies
330 West Olive Street, Suite 100
Milwaukee, WI 53212 USA

Copyright © 2006 by Weekly Reader® Early Learning Library

Managing editor: Valerie J. Weber
Art direction: Tammy West
Cover design and page layout: Kami Strunsee
Picture research: Cisley Celmer

Picture credits: Cover, © Gary Conner/PhotoEdit; pp. 5, 7 Gregg Anderson; p. 9 © North Wind
Picture Archives; p. 11, Unknown, Independence Declared./Mary Evans Picture Library; p. 13
© Gibson Stock Photography; p. 15 © Jeff Greenberg/PhotoEdit; p. 17 © Chris Greenberg/
Getty Images; p. 19 © Tony Freeman/PhotoEdit; p. 21 © AP/Wide World Photos

Printed in the United States of America

1 2 3 4 5 6 7 8 9 10 09 08 07 06

Note to Educators and Parents

Reading is such an exciting adventure for young children! They are beginning to integrate their oral language skills with written language. To encourage children along the path to early literacy, books must be colorful, engaging, and interesting; they should invite the young reader to explore both the print and the pictures.

In *Our Country's Holidays*, children learn how the holidays they celebrate in their families and communities are observed across our nation. Using lively photographs and simple prose, each title explores a different national holiday and explains why it is significant.

Each book is specially designed to support the young reader in the reading process. The familiar topics are appealing to young children and invite them to read — and reread — again and again. The full-color photographs and enhanced text further support the student during the reading process.

In addition to serving as wonderful picture books in schools, libraries, homes, and other places where children learn to love reading, these books are specifically intended to be read within an instructional guided reading group. This small group setting allows beginning readers to work with a fluent adult model as they make meaning from the text. After children develop fluency with the text and content, the book can be read independently. Children and adults alike will find these books supportive, engaging, and fun!

— Susan Nations, M.Ed., author, literacy coach,
and consultant in literacy development

It is the Fourth of July! Do you know whose birthday it is?

4

5

The Fourth of July is the birthday of our country. Our country is the United States of America.

Another country called Great Britain once ruled the United States. On July 4, 1776, the leaders of our country signed a paper. The paper said our country was free from Great Britain.

July Fourth is also called Independence Day. The first Independence Day party was in 1777.

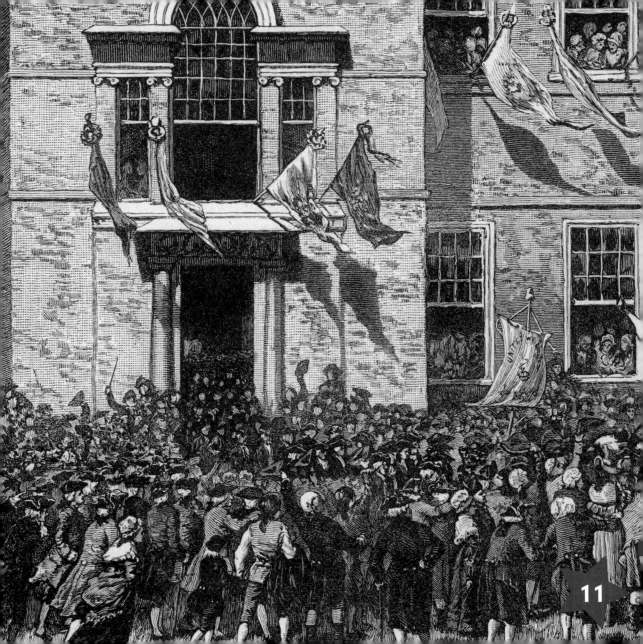

On the Fourth of July, we are glad our country is free. Every year we hold parties to celebrate our country. We watch parades. We put streamers on our bikes and ride in parades.

13

Friends and families hold picnics on July Fourth. There are games and food. The birthday party lasts into the night.

Cities and towns shoot off fireworks at night. Do you like the loud bangs and bright lights?

17

Red, white, and blue are our country's colors. Our flag is red, white, and blue. On the Fourth of July, we use these colors to show we love our country.

18

July Fourth is the day we say "Happy Birthday" to our country! We feel proud to be Americans.

21

Glossary

celebrate — to have a party to honor a special event

country — the land that forms a nation

independence — freedom

proud — very pleased

ruled — had power over someone or something

22

For More Information

Books

Happy Birthday America. Mary Pope Osborne
(Roaring Brook Press)

Independence Day. Holidays (series). Julie Murray
(Buddy Books)

Independence Day. Let's See Library (series).
Marc Tyler Nobleman (Compass Point Books)

Independence Day. Rookie Read-About Holidays
(series). David F. Marx (Children's Press)

Web Sites

Fourth of July History
www.holidays.net/independence
Fun facts and activities about Independence Day

23

Index

About the Author

Sheri Dean is a school librarian in Milwaukee, Wisconsin. She was an elementary school teacher for fourteen years. She enjoys introducing books and information to curious children and adults.

24